BLIZZARD

Blizzard

MATTHEW FRANCIS

FABER & FABER

First published in 1996
by Faber & Faber Ltd
Bloomsbury House, 74–77 Great Russell Street, London WC1B 3DA

Revised edition published in 2016

Typeset by Faber & Faber Ltd
Printed and bound in Great Britain by TJ Internationsl Ltd.

© Matthew Francis, 1996, 2016

Matthew Francis is hereby identified as author
of this work in accordance with Section 77
of the Copyright, Designs and Patents Act 1988

A CIP record for this book
is available from the British Library

ISBN 978-0-571-33114-7

10 9 8 7 6 5 4 3 2

To Dan with best

for Creina

wishes

Matthew Francis

Acknowledgements

Acknowledgement is due to the following publications, in which some of these poems first appeared: *Bright Star, City Writings, The Forward Book of Poetry* (1994), *Harvest '92, Home and Away, Outposts, PN Review, Poetry Introduction 7, South, Stand, The Stony Thursday Book*. A selection was published as a pamphlet under the name *Towards Midnight* (Scratch, 1995).

The poem 'Occupied City' is based on accounts from Ernst Jünger's diaries, first published as *Gärten und Straßen* in 1942 and now as part of the *Sämtliche Werke* edition (Klett-Cotta, Stuttgart, 1979).

I should like to thank the following for their advice and encouragement: my wife Creina, my brother Richard, and members of Winchester Poetry Workshop and Wykeham Poetry. I should also like to thank Ernst Jünger for his kind permission to publish 'Occupied City'.

Contents

Beestorm in West Middlesex

He sat in the solemn office.
It was a poem about bees.
The room was silent and the air
full of unwritten thunder.

It was a poem about bees.
The room was silent and the air
full of unwritten thunder.
The bees exploded on the window-pane.

The room was silent and the air
full of unwritten thunder.
The bees exploded on the window-pane,
a living wreath around the trees.

Full of unwritten thunder,
the bees exploded on the window-pane,
a living wreath around the trees,
which then dispersed like memories.

The bees exploded on the window-pane,
a living wreath around the trees,
which then dispersed like memories.
He sat in the solemn office.

It was a poem about bees.

After the Bee

It must have been one of the last bees.
It clung to my wrist with its hook feet,
unshakeable, almost comatose,
an unspectacular forest bee,
a shivering burr of black and white.
Then it stung me

and I picked it wriggling off its sting
and dropped it like a nut on the path.
I felt the place, already growing
a sprout of pain. It was nothing much,
more news from the outside, but my breath
couldn't quite reach

my brain suddenly and I walked on
I walked on into the sunlit trees,
the slats of light and dark. I sat down
on something that wasn't there. I sat
down again and listened to the buzz
of a last thought

a last thought leaving its empty hive
for the winter. The leaves were falling
up, down and round. I watched one revolve
in the air as if it had no need
to go anywhere. I rose, feeling
my way upward

and climbed up into the canopy
where all the leaves were that didn't fall.
Below me the crinkled forest lay
turned by small creatures. I was there too,
my body lying on the ground, still,
stingless, hollow,

not mine after all, killed by a bee.
So this was what I had always feared.
It wasn't like dying. I could see
behind all those noises that you hear
on walks: that rustle was a blackbird,
that sigh a deer

taking off through the tree corridor
that only they can find. Who'd come back
through the passage from that soft elsewhere?
I was there now. It started to rain,
vaguely, like a feeling. Someone spoke.
I was lost in

the inside of the forest. They rolled
my sleeve up and stung my arm again.
Shadows stood round me. One of them held
my head. A slight shock. You'll be all right.
Behind them the trees stood, stiff, like men
prepared to wait.

A Blind Man in the Forest

Yes, I know we're in the open now.
There's grass underfoot and the wind is
longer. Let's sit down. I liked it, though,
in the trees. It was a good, loud place
with plenty of crackling. Did you see
the deer? There it was, going away.

That's the best thing about coming here:
the scenery doesn't wait to be
looked at. It gets on. Today the air
was full of falling. I couldn't see
the leaves coming, so they touched my face
like that, with the forthright gentleness

of a child's hand borrowing my thigh
to help himself on to a train once.
I can smell autumn. The woods are high
and the sun hovers on my hands, tense.
It's friendly still but not intimate.
Water is mixing it somewhere. Let's sit

on these flowers you say are like stars,
very small ones, in the close-cropped grass.
Softer than the stars one remembers,
less prickly. Touchable, though. I miss
distant things. Stars are just an idea.
I live at arms' length. I feel my way

to where I am. I don't even see
darkness. I have nothing to look through.
So I let the forest come to me,
like that deer, and go when it wants to.
Without walls it's an enormous place,
oneself. It's as big . . . as big as this.

Again

A horse was grazing on a dome-shaped hill.
I found myself in a strange place I knew.
The yellowed thicket and the trees were still.

I knew the hawthorn, the choked stream, the shrill
unplaceable cry above, the branch askew.
A horse was grazing on a dome-shaped hill

on grass dusty with heath and tormentil.
Leaves shuffled by my side. A magpie flew.
The yellowed thicket and the trees were still –

there must have been a wind to cause that chill
but nothing seemed to flutter as it blew.
A horse was grazing on a dome-shaped hill

as if it was just waiting there until
I got the point, patient, as I pushed through
the yellowed thicket, and the trees were still.

And next time I come back perhaps I will
at last remember what they want me to.
A horse was grazing on a dome-shaped hill.
The yellowed thicket and the trees were still.

Diversion

We drove back from the forest. The car
closed in around us, suddenly full
of yellow scent, the apricot smell
of the chanterelles we had picked there.

And our headlamps picked at the verges,
unravelling hedgerows, leafing through
the dead of the kerbside that were now
exhibits of ragged fur, smudges

we left in sweeping on. Then a sign
stopped us at the crossroads and we turned
right, rattling into nowhere, and ground
through the wrong shadows of a long lane.

Illegible landscapes. And we'd thought
we knew the place backwards. It seemed here
we'd found the dark side of Winchester –
a pretend pub, fields too big to fit

the space we'd left in our minds for them.
Then we were on a hill looking down
at the home-made stars of a strange town,
a concave swirl of lights. On the rim

we saw ourselves from above, wild lights
that grew on their own, golden, self-willed.
And here we were to reclaim them, filled
with the smell of today, apricots.

From a High Place

We saw the hills from the road. From here
they didn't seem too high. Black, not blue,
they looked industrial, a bizarre
huddle of rocks. When we got closer
   they vanished. We were now
climbing the horizon. Steep tangles
scrambled between the bends. Trees grew
        at wild angles.

We parked the car in a clinging town
with the sun on its bare head. Hotels
squeezed in on one side of the street. Noon
on Sunday. We walked up a deep lane
   smothered in summer frills.
It took just two to straggle. We ground
our footsteps into the others. Hills
        have to be earned.

Then when you reach the top you can say
it was worth it, wasn't it? You can,
but no one can hear you. This country
grows mostly wind. 'Takes your BREATH AWAY!'
   There's so much going on
in high places. Maybe I felt fear.
The feeling didn't seem to be mine
        but everywhere.

I can't take too many fields at once.
It's like an ache outside. There's no room
in the mind for all that sky. The greens
modulate soundlessly, the distance
   is written in cold steam.
Cloud-shadows cross the land like someone
walking over its grave. Watching them,
        we rested on

the grassy edge rooted in nothing.
Blackberries grew there, the gorse stickled,
and it seemed to be used for grazing.
It was warm with our heads down, lying
    under the wind, cradled
within the rock of the sky, and there
a spider was twirling down. It held
        a thread of air.

Tuba Mirum

The sky is trumpet yellow on the hills,
lined with their green and ceremonial felt.
Today is louder than it needs to be.

There is the taste of trumpets in the air,
an oil of trumpets from their glamorous necks.
There is the sheen of something almost here

which if you rubbed it into the right earth
might do the dead some good, might open up
a little shoot of breath, like daffodils.

Poem Without Words

An afternoon in early you know
it has birds in it the time of year
they're always writing about things grow
the whatever shines. I'm sitting here
trying to read on the patio
and the thing I mentioned earlier
is on the chimney the flying thing
you notice them about now whistling.

They say it never does the same song
twice or is it that no two ones do
the same one as each other? They sing
in their own languages so they know
which is which. It almost means something.
Evening is coming. Before I go
inside I want to finish this – what
the breeze is reading with me. It's shut.

Where have I got to? They're all the same
these these. It was the Swiss artist friend
did it if there was one. No not him
the woman with the pearls and they found
a pearl in the man's suit in the hem
of his hm. Perhaps I'll read the end.
Perhaps I have. I don't want to know
who did it. Who did they do it to?

And now my black visitor is here
rubbing her pointy face against me
like a boy-whatsit starting a fire.
What do you want then? She doesn't say
the one vowel she knows. Do you want your
stuff that comes in a tin? Actually
she'd rather get her hooks into that
small flies it likes to sing you know it

is flexing the usual turns of phrase
on the rooftop but with a new twist.
Today is going inside. Small flies
are stuttering in what is the last
and most elusive light. There it is
again. You know when I heard it first
I must have been oh. Too dark to read
now. It makes you think. Blackbird, blackbird.

The Guest

Yes, I saw one once, she said. At least,
I suppose it was. I was alone
in this part of the house, a bit lost
in it still. It was late afternoon

and late November. Tea was late too.
The chairs stiffened in the drawing-room.
It was chilly. I got up to go
to the warm kitchen to remind them,

through the long passages with their draughts,
their weather-fronts, echoes, a stray smell
of scent, curry or cheese. The few lights
barely softened the dark. I can't tell

any more where I went wrong. It's changed
now I know the house. Sometimes I try
to find that winter corner, the damp tinged
with a strangeness I can't taste today.

One door was leaking light, underlined
as if I was supposed to notice.
We couldn't afford that. I opened –
what shall I call it? – an inner place

like somewhere inside a paperweight.
A glow bronze as a chrysanthemum,
a man smoking a gnarled cigarette
that curdled the lamplight in a room

warmed by a one-bar fire. He sat there
reading, not looking up. An old man,
intent. He hadn't heard me. Not sure
whether to speak, I stood watching, then,

ever so gently, left him to it.
That was my ghost – or I hope it was.
It scares me more to think someone might
just be living here. It's a big house.

Poem Found in a Box
of Indoor Fireworks

Stunted days of early winter,
lawns abbreviated by
verges of precocious twilight.
Snow not scheduled in the sky,

just the old December weather
fizzling on the patio.
All the potentates of Christmas
left their gifts two days ago.

But there's one last oriental,
bird-eyed, formal, head askew,
peering from his nest of wrinkles.
He has brought an offering too.

He's the genie of the fireworks –
not the fierce November sort
but the docile winter species,
F. domestica, in short.

How he knows your turkey relics,
curried plates incensed with spice,
cartilage and spurned sultanas,
hardened grains of saffron rice.

Possibly you know his cousins,
cracker-mottoes, devilish
geometric plastic puzzles,
fortune-telling microfish

(insignificant blue slivers
which contort upon your palm,
gazing eyeless at your future,
doing backflips of alarm).

Close yourselves inside the curtains
and curtail the lunchtime gloom.
Let the darkness preen and rustle,
stretch its wings inside the room.

Serried in their festive packing,
all the patent fireworks wait,
foil façades and wands and wadding
steeped in secret fulminate.

Light the first one. Watch it smoulder,
on the smeary saucer make
sparkles, ominous aromas.
Look, a splurge of molten snake!

Hong Kong Jack, the smoking sailor,
puffs his stiff fuse smuttily,
and the haunting scent entwines you
of expiring PVC.

Now anticipation flickers
as you watch the next one burn,
creep into an ash confection
like a black and crumbling fern.

Emblems transmutate to embers.
Several differ just in name.
Too few fiendish Bengal matches
spitting green-eyed sherbet flame.

Twelve-part fugue on burning paper,
hardly bright enough to see,
charring into oily strata,
saucer archaeology.

Did you hope for Roman candles
on a candlestick? Indoors?
Did you really think that Guy Fawkes
could come after Santa Claus?

Let me tell you about gardens,
then you may perhaps forgive.
They are fine for flowers and bonfires
but indoors is where you live.

Indoor fireworks cast no shadows.
Only you, not they, may seethe,
but they make you make some darkness
where you hear each other breathe.

You have called another genie
to your table in the dark,
eyes and jewellery all attention,
waiting on his every spark.

This (or suchlike) is The Moral,
not quite tangible but there,
like the afterthoughts of sparklers
singed in orange on the air.

Winter City

We were all tourists. None of us lived here.
It's a long walk from the station to the town
and further still by bicycle, the tick
of turning wheels measuring Hills Road back
to the past – as I knew it was even then.
It's a long life from these streets to any-year.

Hence the self-consciousness, the scarf flaunting
of all those people who didn't yet exist
and were making the most of it, a game
of being young and old at the same time.
Crumpets, port, midnight scrawls. Ducks in the mist,
an unlikely dawn chorus. The pumps grunting,

draining the punting pool for a suicide
who'd jumped from a St John's window, an end
that fulfilled one of the commoner ambitions.
There was an epidemic of impatience
and he decided to become a legend
if not in his lifetime, only just outside.

Perhaps not bright, he did fall from the air.
(It was Tom Nashe's college.) Already ghosts
were everywhere and now a new one coiled
among the wispier vapours of the old,
an after-gate-hours song in empty streets.
If I become one too, it won't be here.

Unless I'm one already without knowing.
There are bits of me I hardly recognize,
looming out of the steam like vague garments
in a deserted drying room where vests,
half-man, half-dragon, hang before the eyes.
The brief-clad pipes clamber above me, coughing.

Winter. Ice in the milk. Writing a poem
where windows stared at windows, I got nearer
to the fire, spreading essentials in the heat
until it fused my jar of Coffee-Mate.
My clock, roosting on a live record-player,
shrieked its alarm each morning at full volume

but punched holes in the night with its hoarse *tock*.
I lay awake thinking of Chinese food.
Only Spenser could put me to sleep. Next day
I got up at four to finish an essay.
The library always smelled of marmalade.
Some heavies were playing rugby with a book.

The Gawain-Poet, metaphor and wit
were sunk in a study, in John Stevens's room.
An emblem or a symbol, something, rolled
under the blue propulsion of its mould
on to the carpet. 'Ah, I've found my jam!'
Outside, the Twinings twilight was poured out.

Then the dark gulped it down and in the air
there was the smokiness of misery,
for it was by the waters of Lapsang
that I lay down and wept. A Dylan song,
weak words, and something hardly hoped, and tea.
Can I still taste the tannin of despair?

Earl Grey on Desolation Row. A friend
declared all women bourgeois. I don't know.
They never lived up to their glamorous rooms,
that dampness I now only smell in dreams,
the basement flats that had a mineral glow,
the walls sponging up odours like a bed.

My bed was hardly big enough for me.
The only odours in it were my own,
and the pain was my own. It isn't now.
You can't inherit from a different you
the things you used to feel about someone
not yours. I, who belonged to nobody,

used to complain I didn't even exist,
flat on the carpet after too much beer.
Now I remember. It was almost me,
a doorway figure I still sometimes see
stepping outside into the winter air
as a gasfire sunset shivers and goes out.

Cirrus Day

The tense watermeadows
were waiting for winter
as we argued clouds
and boats and moorhens.

Ice cobwebs clung to the sky
as we argued
cumulonimbus, altostratus,
the one that looks like fishskin,

how weathermen divide the sky
into eight parts, how poets
had never seen them
as we saw them now,

or rather, then.
They recede so rapidly.
That was a cirrus day,
frozen and frail

and far away.

Occupied City

Laon, France, June 1940

I. THE CATS

We came to the city and found
only the cats were left
to guard the twilight courtyards
with their colourless flowers,
roses, geraniums,
with no one to tend them.
I ordered patrols in the streets.
All looters would be held
in the castle dungeon till morning.

I made my rounds in the dark.
I knew the high street by
the smell of decay from the butcher's
and a café when my torch
lit on a half-full glass.
I potted the last ball
left on the billiard table.

And here was the *Poste de Police*
with a document still in the typewriter
broken off in mid-word
causing a thief whose name
began with Q to go free.
I ripped the paper out
and let it flutter down.
There is no law in defeat.

And there is no law for cats
but a scream in the street,
the fiercest sound in town.
Their war is rotting meat
and no one giving them milk.

I suppose that must be why
they kept following me.
Any human will do.
And yet it was hard not to think
they were on the other side.
They have reasons of their own
to shimmer into a run,
to scowl at something unseen,
to slip into the mouth of a shop,
or to settle in front of me
in the dusty beam of my torch
and try to lick it off.

2. THE CATHEDRAL

Next morning a herd of stone
reared up at me in the sun.
There are white oxen
on the medieval towers,
and a hippopotamus
(nineteenth-century)
thrusts out unexpectedly
above the west door.

I climbed a tower and rested
my hand on the head of a wolf
mangy with yellow lichen.
An eagle, a bat, a lynx,
some devils and a drunken monk
gazed with me over the plain.
Whoever made these figures
knew what a fiend looks like,
his tongue between his teeth,
fearer and feared at once.
The armies were moving again.
A long slate-grey column

shuffled along the main road.
The aeroplanes from here
were no fiercer than the swifts
that tore at nothing below.

I thought of my muttering guards
patrolling the nave inside,
blotched by the rose windows,
talking no doubt of women,
one they had left behind
or one they hoped to find
in the supine republic.
The sacred is just a light
that sometimes stains the skin
of the old profane faces.

I put my hand on these faces
crusted with dried-up green
and warmed to them, as the sun
must so often have done.
I remembered Rimbaud's line
about Europe's parapets
as I leaned on one that might
have been carved out of the air,
overseeing the fields
by some seigneurial right –
that of just being here –
and I wished that the great towers
were suddenly very small
so I could hold them
as one holds someone else's child,
with a sort of courteous love.

3. I LOVE TO GROW OLD

My two officers and I
stayed up late in the cellar
invading Burgundy,
holding a precarious candle
to read labels sideways.
Nothing makes wine taste better
than damp and cobwebs,
hot wax and softening flame.
It was like drinking history.
I remembered that summer,
1934,
and now I drank it again,
filtered through six winters
but still too young.
We all admired the label,
j'aime à vieillir,
I love to grow old,
but now it never would.

I tried to borrow some sleep
the way I had borrowed a bed.
But when I'd got halfway
I had to go back for my feet
which seemed to be borrowed too,
they were so hot and dry.
Suddenly needled awake
I got up and searched the room
for an insect made of air.
How can you kill a creature
that doesn't even exist?
And how can nothing sing
so deep inside the ear?
And then at last it was there
splay-legged on the wall
inviting the blow to fall.

A blow deep in the night
woke me up again.
I thought at first it was thunder.
As I scrabbled out of sleep
someone was slapping the sky
and the clouds were snapping like flags.
But that grinding crunching noise
that followed was underneath
or all round or inside.
It was like a dentist's drill
but the tooth was the whole world.
All the hard things in the world,
rocks and buildings and bones,
were part of one skeleton
the bombs were wrenching apart.
I should have gone to the cellar
but I hated to think of those bottles
shattered and bleeding round me,
turning the dust to red mud.
Then I went back to sleep
and was shaken at intervals,
until I suddenly woke
to the chime of the clock downstairs,
a long rococo peal
tingling with joy in the dark.

4. THE PEN

Having to write a letter
I went to look for a pen.
In the castle I found rifles,
broken chairs, wine casks,
bicycles and jars of jam
scattered like a flea market
overturned by the wind.
In the museum, a copy

of Rubens by Delacroix,
a still life given to the town
by Napoleon III –
peaches and asters in a raw sun,
a blue iris in shadow.
In the library, an edition
of the *Monumenti Antichi*
which took up a whole bookcase,
letters in gracious handwriting
from eighteenth-century botanists,
notes from Eugène Beauharnais
and from Napoleon's doctor.
I couldn't find a pen.

In the law courts I entered
a grand room where I found
on the green cloth of the table
all the judges' wigs.
I sat in the President's seat
and studied the dossier
of an interrupted trial.
But there was no pen.
I climbed a great staircase
and was slightly out of breath
when I reached the President's office
so I sat at his desk for a rest.
The drawers were full of letters,
the shelves cluttered with jars
of pills and medicine bottles.
At last I found a pen.
Now I could have gone back,
but I was too far in
so I explored rooms that smelled
of forgotten days at school,
pencil shavings and rubber,

the sullenness of ink,
rooms where the sunlight lay
waiting to be swept up.
I opened a blue-covered folder
and read the account of a trial
from 1863.
It made me think of Q
who had dissolved in the night,
and then night came again
and dissolved those pages too,
and I returned with my pen.

But when I came to my room
I forgot what I had to write,
so I wrote these words instead
as a way of postponing sleep.
But I think I shall go there now.
It's a great plain like the one
I saw from the tower.
You can find all Europe there:
soldiers and refugees,
rivers and cornfields and rocks,
vineyards and libraries –
they all dissolve into one.
I'm glad I was sent here
to see a town as it sleeps.
There is nothing more intimate
than to offer the world your breath
and close your eyes on it.

01.30. More bombs.

after Ernst Jünger

Friday Street

As I went down to Friday Street
the sun was bright in the sky.
The sky was bright in its circle,
the circle of my eye.

As I went down to Friday Street
the sun was a hammer of gold.
The gardens were open like oysters
when their molten bodies unfold.

And the flowers when I went down there
trembled in purple and blue
and the sun hammered dust from their petals.
There were people I thought I knew:

a man in the door of a bookshop,
a man in a shining suit,
a mother pushing two babies.
Someone was playing a flute.

The woman who asked me directions
was lost in the heart of July
and cars with determined expressions
passed expeditiously by.

Two men, two women, two babies,
and one with the sun in his brain
in a narrow passage of Friday
that opened then closed again.

It's November on the road northwards.
The door to the bookshop is shut.
All the people have vanished like spiders.
Friday is over. But

elsewhere, a Friday evening
is turning the flowers grey
and through the 9 p.m. gardens
a flute is picking its way.

Winter Road

Driving along the road
I see the black wires
that held the leaves together,
how summer's trick was done.

England always reverts
to winter. We've given up
trying to be elsewhere.
The sky is just a breath

away from the hills.
The mist of the morning stretches
to touch the evening mist.
I feel about to find

something the huddled blues
and greys have been hiding.
The small steep fields are like
banks to the hairline streams.

The ponies won't stand still.
They tear at the stiff grass
and then shimmy away.
The world takes some eating.

What if the blue is just
exhaust? The air is hung
with a sourness from the earth.
Steam from some poison stew?

I know there's no reason
to love the soil. It has
worms, not feelings, bones
and shells for memories.

Yet now I'm surprised
by its breath on the windscreen,
a dark that knows its business
closing over the road.

The land was here first.
If you could want a thing
to outlast all wanting,
I'd want it to be after,

but as it is, I hope
I'll always sense that breath
beyond the winter verge.
I hope it stands its ground.

Power Cut

Where did the time go? The clocks went out.
Candles are busy in all the rooms.
We move from zone to zone, still sometimes
reaching for the light switch. We forget

even though we know, as when someone
dead almost comes down the stairs before
you can stop him. No, there's no one there.
Neighbours are talking in the garden –

we didn't know we had so many.
Their voices crisscross, passing between
hedges, as their cats do. Did you phone?
And did they tell you what they told me?

We are alone, with only people
for company, and the various
insects that share our houses with us
and the long whiskers of web that feel

the dark and the candles' new-laid light.
There must be, there is a connection.
The torch-beams out in the substation
are jostling now, trying to find it.

In the Birds' Wood

A town with no outside
whose streets are secret.
They have the names of forests:
Birdswood Drive, unpeopled,
unconscious road. Outside
in the untemperature
is nowhere. Inside
the family romance,
the classic serials.
Now we are talking
shadows. Episode one,
warm fruit, sun
on the porch. Surely,
my dear fellow, nihilism?
And at your time of life.
I have been fourteen
for several years,
kneeling on the carpet
behind curtains
in the rose blue dark.
I have come down to watch
a girl become a woman
at the open window,
the night air swelling,
storms of moths drumming
episode one, summer,
shadows of love
in the gooseberries,
a boot-toe biting the grass.

For those who missed it,
we have been talking shadows.
Outside it is Birdswood,
Hermitage Wood,
as was. The streetlamp,
ticking, is planning something.
A car clears its throat,
and the tall straight-haired model
is walking her Alsatian,
walking shadows,
dwindling and growing,
lamp-post to lamp-post.
Episode four. She threatens
her husband in a nightgown.
Her breasts by candlelight
move him to tears.
Dorset is gripped by consumption.
Her back arches, sweat forms
adulterous droplets.

By episode six
it is all over –
moth-storms, carpets, skin
dappled and shifting,
cars arriving at midnight
having been nowhere,
the meeting under the beeches,
horses, heads bowed, whispers.
A town without history
remembers nothing: unconscious
air, pavement, streetlamps,
birds, leaves.

The Inferno of Ascupart Street

There is such a place,
ruled by a legendary demon
with Hampshire connections.
I've just missed an appointment

and here there is no light
except what's left in the lemons and grapefruit
of one late stall
to remind me of Paradise –

and gleams between the shutters of sex shops.
Miles of council flats
are calling like an estuary.
The sea is not to be found.

Tuesday is closed for the winter.
The green arcades
are filling with muttering shadows.
The bus will be a long time coming.

Notes for a Nightingale

Effects of leaves and lights. On my way home.
    Town to myself. Feeling of space. Maybe
a car goes past or possibly there's some
    drunk hurrying to get away from me.
I cross the street and sit on a warm wall.
    Describe the garden. Smells of honey, soap.
        The mixed grey flowers and the springy way
            the spikes of grass uncurl
although you never see what curled them up.
    Bird sings in tree above, a cherry, say.

Surprise at hearing, or at any rate
    that I know straight away what it must be.
Continuous, not blackbird. Delicate
    crescendo. *Song: lu lu lü lü le leee.*
Breeds woods and parks. Plate on page 259.
    Prefers damp undergrowth. (Not cherry trees?)
        Not often seen. (This one's invisible.)
        Sings a few weeks in June.
Like being in a poem. Full-throated ease.
    One of those things you read before you feel.

Images: water crossed with something sweet
    to show I like it. Syrup? But it's loud.
The kind of syrup that can wake a street.
    Thou wast not born for sleep, insomniac bird.
Lemonade? Sparkling wine? I wonder why
    the sound must always be translated to
        the drinkable. Perhaps to make believe
            it pours itself for me.
I could call it a love song, but with no
    words or composer. Not a human love.

Not often seen. The voice inside the leaves.
　　As if the leaves were speaking. Beautiful
bodiless otherness that only lives
　　for ever by not being visible.
The voice I hear this passing night does not
　　communicate. And passes. And a bird
　　　　is just a softened lizard that can sing.
　　　　　　You can't make sense of that.
　　You can't even believe it once you've heard
　　　　these complications. They must mean something.

Notes for a poem that I want to make
　　to put a bird in I've already found
where else but in a poem? Midnight walk
　　through bird-shaped spaces that I understand
because I read them earlier. And yet
　　the walk did happen. I sat on the wall,
　　　　a grey tree sang, and I was sure somehow
　　　　　　that what I heard tonight
　　or what I thought, my scraps of nightingale,
　　　　would be of use. Perhaps they will be now.

A Nocturnal

The kitchen's full of the north wind.
    You wouldn't want to live there, shivering
on a blue-tiled island
without heating. We leave the oven on
    so that the fan half-hides the hurrying
of the outer darkness forcing its way in.
    Too wild for cooking.

Something is stirring the Christmas cards
    as if they're planning to go off somewhere,
their sails catching the trades.
You cannot always keep the weather out.
    It has a prior claim to everywhere,
especially now, the most voluminous night
    of the whole year.

I have been reading Donne again,
    how she enjoys her long night's festival,
wondering if he felt when
he wrote it some slight pleasure in the dark.
    There was more of it then, and it was real,
and, of course, not. A woman's face was like
    a dwindling candle.

We don't need candles any more.
    There is a decorativeness about
such fiddly, personal fire,
a Laura Ashley peasant radiance.
    We haven't got the corridors for it,
the bare rooms to hang shadows in, the gowns
    to match the light.

And Sweden has eleven wolves,
    and the North Pole is melting far away,
and as the night dissolves,
running down greenhouse walls, the featherscape
    emerges of a snowless winter day.
And yet we load the house up like a ship
    and put to sea

with maps that we've inherited
    from those who needed them. So let's sail on
lamp-lit and spirited
into the heart of darkness. Only there
    on a black background something bright can shine,
the parrot and pistachio can share
    their opened green.

Outside My Window

In the shaped darkness where I used to be,
something is shouting. I'm awake. The voice
is a girl swearing in the not-quite place
you have to cross to get back home to day.

It is a place that wants to be elsewhere.
You never think about it till one night
you leave the pub or party, and the street
is stretched out waiting for you. It is here,

empty and cold, your sleeping theatre,
rinsed with a lamplit silence which you share
with everyone who's stood out here before.
Some bastard starts to play a bass guitar.

Sounds like he's playing over the telephone,
a hollow basement music that you feel
rather than hear. Ponderous. Comical.
You'll be all right in a minute. You'll just lean

on somebody's gatepost till you get your breath
back, while the houses stand not holding theirs.
You clench your jacket, ready. This is yours,
this stretch of midnight, to do something with.

It is a long receptacle of shouts.
Now you feel better, don't you? Now they know,
the upstairs dreamers, that you live here too.
Your words run naked through their curtained nights.

And then you go home and you go to sleep.
The whole town sleeps together, except them,
those hoarse, white memories you can't unscream.
They stand outside your house and wake you up,

you being me. Now it's years later. The face
is someone else's but the same words still
wrench it apart. What are they after? Well,
they've done with me now and I want some peace.

I'm heading for the other side of what
I take to be a sort of game reserve
full of bird-noises and the whining of
that bug the milk-float settling on the street.

Where You Are

In a hotel, in a seaside town,
in France, beside me in a strange bed,
but most of all, asleep. You have gone
into the distance that everyone
    carries around inside.
Your breath comes from far away, like smoke
from towns glimpsed from a crest in the road.
        What is it like

to live there? Do you have work to do?
By the sound of it. You have no time
for anything except breathing now
until the wind changes and you go
    about, hoisting an arm
to catch a pressure I cannot feel.
There is no sound but you in the room
        and it seems full

of you, as though you were projecting
your mind on the faint walls. As for me,
I'm just here, unstowable, twitching,
too long for my limbs, crumpled, watching
    the darkness going by.
I'm stuck till daylight. The street outside
is empty of singing and only
        a smell of bread

comes through the window, as if the room
were thinking of tomorrow. The taste
will follow the smell for you, a dream
and a day with a crust between them.
    Between me and breakfast
there's nothing at all, only I'm here
to see it happen. How have you lost
        yourself, and where?

In seaside towns the dawn chorus is
supplied by gulls. They're scratching about
now, waking and warming up, a mess
of squirming. Soon their scissoring cries
     will stir you. What is it
they make me think of when I hear them?
I don't know if it's a setting out
              or coming home.

Chasak

*These Three Kings offered to our Lord incense,
gold and myrrh . . . they met together in a city
of India which is called Chasak . . .*
              The Travels of Sir John Mandeville

After a month, it stopped. The star
held a stone city in its light.
Intimate with the gleaming streets,
it shook the crouchers on the wall,
tangling their sleep with cries of women
from the night tenements of Chasak.

We, Lord Proclaimer of Chasak,
having in mind the present star,
declare unto all men and women
that its regalities of light
falling at large within the wall
exact the worship of the streets.

There were star-parties in the streets
of the bright corners of Chasak.
Shadows of turret, pillar, wall
were laid out for them by the star.
The novelties of dark and light,
the guttering bare feet of women.

The foreign quarter, beggars, women . . .
Nobody knows me in these streets.
My packs in the inn are stuffed with light.
The gold is resting in Chasak,
waiting for something. And the star
pens both of us inside the wall.

Caspar was sulking on the wall,
losing his retinue. The women
drew his men inside when the star
brightened and bean-smoke twined the streets.
They speak our language in Chasak,
ten languages. Something . . . A light!

In the black desert, blowing, a light.
The warmth of horses. On the wall,
shivering, his hands clasping Chasak,
he heard the nasal songs of women
and the last laughter in the streets.
Who is it coming? Where next, star?

In the remaining light the women
clung to the wall in the cold streets,
Chasak, beached by the ebbing star.

Towards Midnight

Some are born to sweet delight,
Some are born to endless night.

This time the bus stopped for good. Something
had got into the engine, darkness
perhaps. At any rate the choking
began just as we left the empty
almond-blossom streets of the Palace
suburb. Now it was almost country

and almost night we were almost there.
The road juddered and grew whiter. Soon
the grains of twilight formed in the air,
fidgeting like gnats. The fields were soft
and furrowed, for planting footprints in.
And then we stopped. Only two miles left.

Nobody wanted to leave the bus.
The driver shrugged. Our cigarettes glowed
with our attention, whispered to us
as we huddled cheered by the home smell
of brown bags crammed with this morning's bread.
Now we could look round, open a smile.

'Been shopping? You have come a long way.
I suppose the bread is better here.
Are there shortages in your country?
Do you like the sun? I see you all
wear dark glasses. No, never before.
I look forward. You speak English well.'

The door opened. It was time to go.
The mothers wrapped their children round them.
Most walked like those used to it, who know
life has more walking than arriving.
I kept trying to appraise the gloom.
How foreign was it? Was it growing?

Definitely. Indefinitely.
As we got nearer we got vaguer.
Sketches, shadows, one shadow, then me
among voices, sudden and too close.
Surely we must have crossed the border.
I no longer knew where my skin was,

where the next second was coming from.
'This is nothing. You don't know Hamschen,'
somebody said. I couldn't see him
but he saw me. There must have been light,
enough for reading faces even,
if you just knew where to look for it.

Then distances started to come back.
I could see, not people, but the space
between people. An end to the dark,
a pinprick that grew larger and leaked
dimensions into it. Light? A house?
'That where we getting our papers checked.'

Abkhazia Customs. A plank shed
smeary with yellow light. 'You take pen,
make Hamschen form here,' my neighbour said.
It seemed the building doubled. The same
officials did for both. We wound in
and wrapped ourselves three times round the room.

A convention of moths applauded
the lamp they had come so far to see.
Not much but all there was. Men prodded
babies on the counter, curious
about what was in them. On my knee
I wrestled with the papers. Purpose

of Visit: I have always been int –
no, fascinated, by extremes, or,
well, edges. The north face. The moment
the gulls flag and there is only blue.
Excuse the crossings out. Perhaps here
is terminal. This is the end. No,

Purpose of Visit: say, tourism.
A country's not a metaphor. That's
poetic imperialism.
Those outposts turn out to be real,
gasping with stranded adolescents.
Thule, Easter Island, Archangel . . .

My thigh ached and my form was ruined.
They don't give you space to think on these.
It was too late. They started to wind
down a shutter over the counter.
'But I've only just –.' 'Sorry, we close.'
'For the night? When will it be over?

How will you know?' But they had shut us
out with the moths. 'There is a morning
of a sort,' a man said. 'Breakfast is
sold from a trolley outside. Grilled meat,
flat bread and so on. When it's getting
lightish. You eat and watch the sunset.'

'Thank God you're English.' 'Well, English-ish.'
'And I have to stay here till morning?'
'I wouldn't stay here. Nowhere to wash.
The dark is the only place to shit.
The buggers spend the whole night singing.
Here we go! There's one clearing his throat!'

The travellers began to settle
on the floorboards. They had expected
something. They were expectant people.
The place smelled of coffee suddenly.
Nobody sang but two boys started
a game with stones. I wanted to stay

but somebody took the lamp away.
'They do that,' the room said. 'They have done,'
I told him. This was no place for me,
the stones clicking, the darkness folding
and refolding itself. The ish man
knew a hotel with real lighting.

Tourists stayed there to look at the dark,
but not, it seemed, at this time of year.
We stayed up late drinking rum and Coke,
night in a glass, foreign and too sweet,
not tasting quite right. The vacant bar
sizzled with a blue fluorescent light

like one of those things for zapping flies,
except that the flies seemed to like it.
'Do you come from round here?' 'No one does.
This area is neither one thing.
I was born in Hamschen City, but
of English parents. We kept moving.'

He drank like there was no tomorrow.
There wasn't where he came from. The stuff
is a problem when you never know
whether it's late or early. He wore
a white safari suit, looked as if
he was off to shoot a polar bear,

or I should say bear, plural. The man
knew his onion. If he was a prat,
he might still be a prat from Hamschen.
All I knew of it was Mandeville,
a writer of fables, out of date,
who wrote about Paradise as well

and the cross inside the banana.
For him all countries had a moral.
He claimed the Emperor of Persia,
trying to pick fights with Christendom,
provoked a tactical miracle.
The night fell with its dead weight on him

and all his men. Now the land is dark
and no one knows who lives there, although
the occasional cock-crow, dog's bark
or sound of hoofbeats carries outside.
There is a river that passes through
bearing *evidence*, Mandeville said.

'They've almost cleaned up the evidence
from the river – at least, it's mostly
paper cups, sweet wrappers, cola tins,
the usual outers. And they have cars
rather than horses, in the city
anyway. And as for visitors,

you're all welcome. Ish. Just so long as
you keep spending daylight currency,
buying their T-shirts, tactile statues
and postcards with nothing on the front.
It's all neon in Hamschen City,
just like Las Vegas. The government

has legalized the old touch clubs. Now
they're the only places without light.
There's a black market in curtains too.
Most young people can see perfectly.
It seems their sight was lying in wait
for something to look at. And one day

I suppose they'll solve the atmosphere,
woof! The Hamschen layer will disperse
and then it *will* be a day. But where
will my childhood be? Those dear, long-lost
nights in outer Hamschen with no stars.
You could tell day from night by the taste.

But in the mushroom fields you couldn't
taste your saliva. You could smell them
even indoors, through walls. I haven't
quite got it out of the old pores now.
You ought to visit a mushroom farm.
They grow so fast you can hear them grow.

Gill monsters. They feed on the darkness,
and manure. You can't live in Hamschen
for long without suspecting all this
is for their benefit. They run it,
bastards. I won't eat another one
as long. Call that a plant? Is it shit.

Some aren't even the shape of mushrooms.
Some are like trumpets or stalagmites,
lemon peel, puffballs. And all those forms
so damn smug. Some have a greenish glow.
It's one of the weirdest – only – sights,
a whole hillside with a soft halo,

like an EU quota of green thoughts.
You know what it is they grow them in?
63% of the world's bats
live in Hamschen. We'd be up to here
but for the farms. Rich stuff. And you can
eat the bats, too. Best served slightly rare,

like quails with more oomph. The place to go
for bats is the Endless Night Hotel,
bat *au diable*. Are you booked, too?
You can get rum there that tastes like rum
and they have something of the old style.
Wonderful breakfasts. My God, the time!'

He didn't even look at the clock
so perhaps it was true after all,
he could taste time. At least he could drink
half the night, which may be the same thing.
We shook hands. He left. My glass was full
so I stared into it for a long

half-hour, got up and went to my room.
The passage passed through dinner, stepped down
on to lunch, right, through breakfast and some
exotic disinfectant, then found
a landing whose smell was all its own.
I had my landing in a strange land,

a floor between floors, an odd corner
whose geometry escaped me. Hotels
are full of such crevices, neither
familiar nor quite strange. Key. Open
the door. The room seemed worn out, the walls
scantily papered, the fabrics thin:

chair cover, carpet, bedclothes. Maybe
people had lived harder in this room
and it had room fatigue. Nobody
could weave blankets so frail. And the bed
was so tightly made that every time
I wanted to turn over I had

to ask its permission. I lay there
worrying. First about waking up
in the morning, then about whether
I'd sleep at all. I did, then awoke
to remind myself to go to sleep.
Well, that did it. I'd never get back

to wherever it was I was now.
I didn't dream of mushrooms or bats.
There are places where you cannot go
and still be you, so I'll pass quickly
through those chattering and writhing streets.
I woke feeling it was already

late but somehow early, too. No light
spitted the curtains. The morning was
stealthy, like Christmas. I washed, then fought
my rucksack for my clothes. Strange to think
of Hamschen City where my suitcase
was even now waiting in the dark.

I went outside. Yes, you could taste it.
There was a busyness in the air
and I thought I could smell that grilled meat.
It was crowded. As we pressed forward
to Customs, the sky turned. Slightly rare.
It was morning. The night was ahead.

Small Hours

1

Gently dip, but not too deep
in the treacle-well of sleep.

When the curtains learn to fly,
gently open half an eye.

Gently at the knock of rain
open all the doors again.

Now the clock rings quarter past
something. It is Time at last.

2

One, two, three four five.
Night is only half alive.

Six, seven, eight nine ten.
Time to wake it up again.

Ten, nine, eight seven six.
Back across the River Styx.

Five, four, three two one.
Now look what you've gone and done.

3

Press your ribs against the sheet.
Things are moving in the street.

Who calls old iron door to door?
Someone that you can't ignore.

Clang of iron, cling of rust,
ring the iron angelus.

One, two, three, the shots resound,
but no body will be found.

4

Birds whose voices run with light
shouldn't let it loose at night.

The night-walkers of the town
are sulking in their long black gowns.

All the street signs are in Dutch.
You may see but do not touch.

All the vowels of all the birds
won't congeal into words.

5

Early risers get to know
the wind that makes their shadows blow

and the one red trembling star
where the dark is still ajar,

but if you wake at quarter past
something, you may guess at last

that there's a day inside the night,
curled inward like an ammonite.

Blizzard

How it began. I don't remember.
  They all said it was too cold to snow
but to me it seemed that the weather
  was on the move. There was a chill glow

in the air; sunset was delicate
  and distant. Then it began. I know
it must have, a first flake in the night.

There are no witnesses. In the dark
  when everyone was asleep, too high
and small to notice, the forming flake
  locked up a hint of water while I

may have stirred in my bed. There was no
  whisper, no streak in the curtained sky,
and things do not begin. But they do.

2

In weathergirlspeak, a light dusting
  of snow on the high ground. Here we see
on the satellite that snow edging
  in from the east. It will feel very

she said cautiously. They are angels
  in disguise, looking down. Don't tell me
they've stood in *that wind*, know how it feels.

I woke up next day and it was there.
  I live on the high ground and I saw
it smattered on the street like sugar
  on a cake, so fine a foot would go

straight through to grey, and the roofs edging
  into mountains. Warm at the window
I felt very. Hm. I felt something.

3

Afternoon is its great enemy.
   I could smell meltwater in the air
when I went out. It was a fine day,
   and the snow on the walls turning clear,

thinning to floss. Two boys were trying
   to scrape it into snowballs. There were
some clogged angles to finger, shrinking.

Afternoon is so short. The sun goes
   and leaves nothing to shine but the roads
glazed with the orange lamplight. It *was*
   a fine day, but this winter air needs

a touch of sun to melt it. The sky
   wasn't there suddenly, only clouds
and bits of clouds, the oncoming grey.

4

It snowed off and on. Off was better.
   Leaving the house at night I would tamp
the new front path into place. The car
   hunched in its coating under the lamp

and the exposed moon blued a soft street
   I had to learn again hump by hump –
it seemed a pity to open it.

It snowed on and on with just a glimpse
   of off. At night you could hardly see
how much of it was falling. The lamps
   were pestered by a moth-storm that they

seemed to attract, or create. It fell
   up or down indiscriminately,
and I didn't go out. Out was full.

5

Something was wrong with the weathergirl's
    smile. Now let's take a look at the chart
for mid-day tomorrow, and it tells
    the same story. If you're going out

wrap up, watch out for those hazardous
    driving conditions. The smile. That's it
from me, a very good night. Nervous.

The children were shouting in the park.
    The sound was pitched on the edge of song,
half-curdled into laughter, a shock
    to the suburban air that seemed long

gone a moment after I'd heard it.
    Some quality of snow, something wrong
with my ears? You nerd, Kev. You're dead meat.

6

A railway carriage. Twilight. We'd stopped,
    it seemed, to study a basic field –
the snow, paintbrush trees, pylons, I kept
    reading and rereading till I failed.

Swaying lights, darkness. I'd lost my place
    and fallen asleep. My cheek was cold
on the misted glass. What stop is this?

This is the dance of the waiting-room.
    You shuffle, you fidget, one goes out,
dances his solo on the platform.
    Back in a flurry and stamps his feet

and everyone moves round in a ring.
    They call it the Blizzard Spirit, but
there's always some prat who wants to sing.

7

Dogsnow is always new. It explodes
    when you run in it. The only place
that you can eat and drink, but it bleeds
    when you take it home. It turns your piss

to weather. You can't leave it behind
    however fast you run. And what's this
underneath? No smells to understand.

After a few days the dogs got bored.
    First it was crisp and diggable, then
the shoes got to it, and it was scoured
    down to the raw grass to build snowmen

that shrivelled in their plots. The roads were
    slicked to black, with a crest. In the town
we trod it to frozen milk, and swore.

8

Snow on snow on snow on snow on snow
    Coming down again. Coming down a
I didn't go out. I didn't go
    Lovely weather for geese. Lovely wea

It snowed on and on. It snowed on and
    The falling grey. The falling grey. The
Endless. Endless. Endless. Endless. End

We're talking serious weather now.
    It's been on the news. No more of those
smiling girls. Not just the odd snowplough
    out in force either. Could be the freeze

of the century if it keeps up.
    Maybe a new Ice Age. No one knows.
Doesn't stop them talking. Doesn't stop

9

Now where was I? Standing at the door.
   It was dark again. This evening's snow
had half-filled our footprints. I could hear
   soft voices, an opening window.

Cut off, we watched the lights on the west
   side of town with envy. There were no
stars here, and the road was overcast.

In the republic of candles each
   light is created equal and there
is provision for darkness and such
   spiders et cetera as heretofore

resident. See the margin. You'd be
   surprised what has survived. Let them here,
each according to its lights, run free.

10

It got into the television.
   There was always a loud fuzz between
Michael Buerk and yourself. Chaos on
   The Late Show, hands waving, Tom Paulin

shouting against the wind. Then a blank.
   Then a palm-tree island on the screen,
streaked with unlikely yellow, blue, pink.

So we all turned to each other, not
   knowing who else to believe. They said
it was a just a blip in the climate,
   a volcano, global warming, God.

It had snowed in Zaire. The North Sea
   was frozen. Already the wolves had
crossed to Scotland. They were on their way.

11

Outside Marks and Spencer's they gathered
    with their lanterns for the Festival
of Northern Lights. Their snowmen glittered,
    and their snow women, and a snow whale.

Where had they come from? I hadn't seen
    any of them, these gleamed-on people
in rich fake fur. When did they blow in?

Tattered bonfire flames. An Inuit
    torch song. Then dancing. A fire-eater.
Pagan hymns. Jugglers. The jingling hat.
    The joint passed from glove to glove. Later

we sat in the wet ash dawn and talked
    bears. We slept in the shopping centre
in the slush among the jetsam, wrecked.

12

How I cleared the road to the corner
    with only a shovel. How Jane took
an hour to reach the shops for sugar
    on foot. How Vera served tea and cake

all afternoon. How the milk float came
    at last, in daylight. How we would talk
to the neighbours' children, keep them calm.

And the children weren't scared after all.
    And the milk in the bottles was ice.
And the power failed and the kettle
    was boiled in a shed by Calor gas.

And when she got there it had all gone.
    And the snow stung like grit in my face.
It seems so long ago. Seems such fun.

13

Da da DADA da da DA da. Swit.
  Swirlywhoop. And the whurble will pfee
wubwubwub. Number wub in the chart.
  Da da DADA de toute façon schwee

woo ah bien d'accord when I'm feeling
  woo oo oo oo oo oo ooh. Jetzt sie
witzg einig. Wump. Getting anything?

The friends we shared our homes with have gone.
  Wrapped in blankets in the dark, we still
hoped to hear the heating coming on
  or that the blipping numbers would tell

our time for us. The last voice to go,
  after the TV, was that sad call
of a trumpet on the radio.

14

Organize. We must save energy.
  Insane to starve on our own. House share.
Body warmth. Burn the chairs. You can't be
  a vegetarian now. There are

fields of frozen sheep just down the road.
  Party of six at dawn, and two more
to the shops. Then break in! Take a spade.

Something strange happened today. I found
  a tank in a field. There was no one
in it, of course. Yes, the army kind,
  wedged in a drift with its lid open

like a container for snow. There was
  nothing to steal. When I touched the gun,
which was aimed at the ground, my glove froze.

15

Delicious kernels of farm-grown corn.
    Tender flakes of tuna in a rich
tomato sauce. Children love these fun
    shapes. Lightly herbed cheesy parcels, each

wrapped in a vine leaf. Brush with egg yolk.
    Do not boil. Dust with Parmesan. Poach
10–12 minutes. Use by last week.

There's no label on this tin. Must have
    come off. I had to fight them for it.
It looks naked. Open it. I love
    surprises. A khaki goo a bit

sludgy underneath. It smells spicy.
    Cold and sticky on my finger. Sweet.
Do I like it? What's it meant to be?

16

Once there was a fire and people sat
    in the lap of it. Once mothers held
children between their knees. Once the fat
    of a joint of mutton spat and squealed

and soot and snow scrapped in the chimney.
    Once there were cats and the shadows growled.
Once or twice someone told a story.

I went to piss in the snow outside
    and when I came back in she was there
in the hall. She took my hand and said
    upstairs. It was freezing in the bare

darkness. I held her breasts sculpted from
    gooseflesh. Just as I came inside her
the streetlamp flashed once. Upon a time.

17

It is deep enough now to cover
    almost everything. Going outside
I'm always afraid of the shudder
    of something solid under the spade.

So far only a dog bedded down
    that forgot to wake up, frozen hard.
You need no burial and no stone.

I stood in the breath of the window.
    I was signing my name on the moon.
And down below was the thick fat snow.
    I was going to scrawl on it soon.

There's KILROY WAS HERE on the window
    and it says FUCK YOU JACK on the moon.
But when you blow on the thick fat snow

18

In those days a man stood in the street
    drawing pictures. SIN was a black cloud.
GOD was the sun waiting behind it.
    SIN made us cold, and snow fell, which stood

for itself, I think. It came to pass
    just then anyway and the man fled
without time for PUNISHMENT or GRACE.

Woolworths had metal shutters, a lock
    that had stood up to the hacksaws, but
Boots was strewn with glass. Thorntons smelt like
    the ghost of Easter. What idiot

bothered to steal CDs from Our Price?
    In Waterstones, a lone dustjacket
had been remaindered. You can burn this.

19

You have to watch where you put your feet
    in Firewood Forest. There are burrows,
ponds, bogs of leaf sludge. You can step right
    through the crust into the icy ooze.

Too far from home. You'd never get dry.
    They say there's no pain. The feeling goes
as if slipping your mind. Then you die.

The sticks cracked a joke. A branch coughed snow
    in Firewood Forest. Did someone say
someone said something? Oh, only you
    clearing your throat. It returned to me

as a Chinese whisper. Let's go back
    while we still can. I don't like the way
the ground gleams at me. It's getting dark.

20

There was no birdsong. The only green
    we knew was evergreen. The cats had
no firelight scamperers to jump on.
    Tins were harder to find. All our food

took more of us longer to dig out.
    Rows of stiff houses. The neighbourhood
was drifting downward, street after street.

Foraging by daylight, I could feel
    the burner inside me flicker like
damp firewood fighting for flame. My whole
    body was dead but I could still work

while the wood burned. But my body rose
    from its wet coat at night with a shriek
and walked to the grate where the flame was.

21

I woke up with the sun inside me,
    got out of my sleeping bag and found
I was still in it. When I spoke my
    voice was a long time ago. The sound

was there when I next looked. Finally
    they asked me what was wrong. I explained
I was too cold and too hot. Thirsty.

I woke in the dark. There was the cup
    so I drank it all. Next time I woke
it was full of snow. I had a sip
    and woke to find it empty. I took

a mouthful in case and a draught of
    icy window. Then I had a lick
of the full moon to take the shine off.

22

One hundred and four. I didn't know
    we still had numbers. The same three grave
faces keep coming back. They're here now
    above me nodding as if they have

batteries in them. But what will happen
    when they run down? It's ten thirty-five,
they say. How many ill now? Seven.

I have an ache in my right floorboard
    and it's still snowing behind my eyes.
I told them I see things but they said
    that's normal. How can they tell it is?

A woman comes and polishes me
    with a cold cloth. Why? Is she a nurse?
Or am I a window suddenly?

23

I am lying where I am lying.
  The sun lies on the floor. The floor lies
in the sun. I hear people making
  the noise people make when they make noise.

I can just reach my fingertips if
  I stretch out inside my hands. There is
more of me than I thought. It's enough.

I got better. I laughed stupidly
  when they told me to shush. I drank soup
chasing the globules of fat with my
  spoon. I was let off the washing up.

We lay by a weak fire in daylight.
  They came and went. Sometimes a tall group
stood over someone, working them out.

24

in the town centre. Anyone hurt?
  is all right. It's the smell I can't bear.
the last one. There was less than we thought.
  did it all over the fucking floor.

off his gloves. He's in a lot of pain.
  not too good. It won't be much longer.
hasn't come back. How long has it been?

I don't want to worry you but it's
  I'm not happy about her. Come and
Does anyone know? Don't panic. That's
  Keep your voice down. Now when did you find

Well, don't ask me. I don't know what to
  Go and get Trevor. Say it happened
Look, we did what we could. What will you

25

An hour or so from home, towards night.
    I had found nothing. Halfhearted snow
made its way down. I took a short cut
    through an estate that I thought I knew.

It was commuterland once, golden
    desirable brick. Where was it now?
Here was gone. A strange place had moved in.

The wetflutterhop of snowwalking,
    one upfootsnag after another
when you are dimlost and neckmelting
    flakeshivers sighchill you. Fearglimmer

of a whereamIwhirling plungeshock.
    Now your homecracklelight's greyfurther.
Thoughtflakefalldriftfootsnowfreezecoldlock.

26

They found me at the end of the road
    furled in a snowstorm. They brought me in
and sat me before the fire. Outside
    continued but I didn't listen.

The world was within reach of a flame
    or where you could walk to and return
and still be breathing. I was my home.

And you and you and you. How do we
    bear it when people are there and not
any more? I am too tired to be
    sorry for anyone. Enough heat

is still there in the red for a squirm
    in each other's sleep. The dead are shut
in their ice bedrooms. They can't get warm.

27

Things you can see overhead: woodsmoke,
    clouds, the sun trying to get away,
tomorrow's snow, and what's that? A flock
    of seagulls, the first birds in the sky

since we got small, on their way somewhere,
    storm by storm. Somewhere's the place to be.
Such a lot of it. Sounds like summer.

Things you can see in the fire: a cave,
    mating snakes, daffodils, a balloon,
and what's that spat on the hearth? A live
    beetle, the first land crawler I've seen

in weeks. It must have slept in the bark
    and been defrosted. Now it climbs in
stick by stick back to the unburnt dark.

28

If it thawed now everyone might drown.
    It seems the evenings are growing pale –
it isn't spring, though, or not the green
    perfumey kind. Even that was all

a mix-up. We were just passing close
    to the sun. It wasn't personal.
A rose was a feeling not a rose.

I've got something out of it, if you
    can get things out when there may not be
anywhere different to take them to.
    This is no postcard: weather lovely,

wish I was here. I am, while my luck
    holds and the weather is good to me.
The street is beautiful. Come and look.

29

I took my tin opener, a knife
    and spoon from the kitchen drawer, a spade
for the deeper roads. I wrapped a scarf
    twice round my face and put up my hood.

The moon had just set. A stonewashed sky
    was wearing out as I reached the road
and the swung gate clacked behind me. Bye.

Breakfast was 'borrowed' tuna and snow.
    The sun rose like a boiled raspberry sweet
reddening the motorway below
    with its clumps of dead cars. It led straight

to London. There, if at all, they'd have
    whatever I had meant by the note
I didn't leave. Gone to get help. Love.

30

How it began I don't remember.
    The beginning's shrunk in the past and
the ending glides into the future.
    There is no telling how it will end,

just guesswork. So I have to make do
    with the road to London. Let's pretend
the bells are ringing there for the thaw.

I need this to be complete. There must
    be an answer. Say, a missing word
I've looked for all along that stayed just
    beyond the shovel. Clearing the road,

I stop to rest on my spade. The light
    is hurting, my hands aren't there, my head
becomes the snow suddenly it's white